MAX RICHTER

PIANO WORKS

CHESTER MUSIC

Published by:
Chester Music,

Exclusive Distributors:
Hal Leonard
7777 West Bluemound Road
Milwaukee, WI 53213
Email: info@halleonard.com

Hal Leonard Europe Limited
42 Wigmore Street
Marylebone, London, W1U 2RY
Email: info@halleonardeurope.com

Hal Leonard Australia Pty. Ltd.
4 Lentara Court
Cheltenham, Victoria, 3192 Australia
Email: info@halleonard.com.au

Order No. CH82764
ISBN 978-1-78305-696-5
This book © Copyright 2014 by Chester Music.

Edited by Sam Lung.
Music engraved and processed by Camden Music Services.
Cover designed by Fresh Lemon.
Front cover image © Yulia Mahr.
Images courtesy of Yulia Mahr and Wolfgang Borrs.
With special thanks to Max Richter and Henning Fuchs.

www.halleonard.com

Printed in the EU.

CONTENTS

ABOUT MAX

The work of the award-winning British composer Max Richter includes concert music, film scoring, and a series of acclaimed solo albums.

Working with a variety of collaborators including Tilda Swinton, Robert Wyatt, Future Sound of London, and Roni Size, Max's work explores the meeting points of many contemporary artistic languages, and, as might be expected from a student of Luciano Berio, Max's work embraces a wide range of influences.

Recent projects include the ballet *INFRA*, for Wayne McGregor at the Royal Ballet, with scenography by Julian Opie, the award-winning score to Ari Folman's *Waltz With Bashir*, and the music installation The Anthropocene, with Darren Almond at White Cube.

Max's music has formed the basis of numerous dance works, including pieces by Lucinda Childs, NDT, Ballet du Rhin, American Ballet Theatre, Dresden Semper Oper, the Dutch National Ballet, Norwegian National Ballet, among many others, while film makers using work by Max include Martin Scorsese (*Shutter Island*, 2010) and Clint Eastwood (*J. Edgar*, 2011).

Recent commissions include the opera *SUM*, based on David Eagleman's acclaimed book, premiered at the Royal Opera House, London and Mercy, commissioned by Hilary Hahn.

Other projects include *Vivaldi Recomposed* for Deutsche Grammophon, recorded by British violinist Daniel Hope and the Konzerthaus Orchester, Berlin, as well as a variety of other recording and film projects. Max is currently writing the music for the upcoming HBO drama series *The Leftovers*, created by *Lost* co-creator Damon Lindelof and acclaimed novelist Tom Perrotta.

NOTES FROM MAX

ANDRAS

Andras is the imaginary composer of this music, from my album *Memoryhouse*.
This needs a sense of urgency and intensity as it progresses.

THE BLUE NOTEBOOKS

This is a tiny nocturne. Be careful with the rhythm so that the second beats
always fall in the same way.

CIRCLES FROM THE RUE SIMON-CRUBELLIER

The title refers to the home address of the protagonist in Georges Perec's wonderful work
Life: A User's Manual (La Vie mode d'emploi). The hero of the novel embarks on a somewhat
random circumnavigation as part of the story — therefore 'circles'. The right and left hands
play in different metrical groupings. Steady!

DEPARTURE

This music is from Feo Aladag's powerful film *When We Leave* (*Die Fremde*). The work
accompanies the heroine's brave decision to leave her family and home — it is a sort of
'journey' nocturne. Pay attention to the countermelody in the upper voice of the left hand.

THE FAMILY

This piece comes from the score for Cate Shortland's extraordinary film *Lore*. Towards the end
of the film many of the characters have been lost, and all manner of relationships sundered.
This piece is a little requiem, all built from steady repeated notes.

FRAGMENT

Appearing on my album *Songs From Before*, this piece is a trip through the same harmonic
landscape as 'Leo's Journal'. The left hand employs simple pulsations which, nevertheless,
do have a countermelody in them. The big stretch of a tenth can be taken by the right hand.
Towards the end, take care to ensure the melody crosses cleanly under this.

FROM THE RUE VILLIN

This is from my album *Songs From Before*. The novelist Georges Perec lived at number 24.

H IN NEW ENGLAND

This is a piece of travelling music from the film *Henry May Long*. Pay attention to the inner
voices in the left hand and make sure that the 'three against two' is steady.

HORIZON VARIATIONS

'Horizon Variations' is from my album *The Blue Notebooks*. It needs to be very steady. Make sure that you let the inner voices sing. The second half of the piece can have more tone, as the quaver movement starts.

INFRA 3

This piece is from my album *INFRA*, a version of the ballet score of the same name, which I wrote for the Royal Ballet in 2008. The work is involved with journeying, making much use of material from Schubert's *Winterreise*. In something of a departure, 'INFRA 3' is a homage to his Impromptu in G-flat.

LEO'S JOURNAL

This piece is another trip through the music of 'Fragment'. The left hand needs to be very stable and controlled so that the melody can easily sing over it. The hand crossing at the end should not interrupt the flow.

THE TARTU PIANO

I once travelled overnight during midwinter to the Estonian city of Tartu to play a concert. In the brutalist concrete arts centre there was a wonderful piano for the concert, so I wrote a piece for it.

THE TWINS (PRAGUE)

This little duet is for beginners. It is based on a typical Classical-era Alberti Bass figure (in the left hand), though somewhat subverted. It needs to be very light, unaccented and as fast as comfortable. The melody should be played tenuto and must really sing.

VLADIMIR'S BLUES

This is from my album *The Blue Notebooks*. The 'Vladimir' of the title is the writer Vladimir Nabokov, who (like me) had a keen interest in butterflies and was an expert on the family known as 'The Blues'. Another expert on butterflies was the pianist Walter Gieseking, whose playing of Chopin I much admire; therefore I have borrowed the oscillating right-hand figure from Chopin's Nocturne Op.15 No.1 — the movement is a little like the flapping of wings.

WRITTEN ON THE SKY

This piece is from my album *The Blue Notebooks*. It is an epilogue which reprises the harmonic structure heard at the beginning of my piece 'On The Nature Of Daylight'. The music should remain mobile, and mustn't be heavy.

ANDRAS

MUSIC BY MAX RICHTER

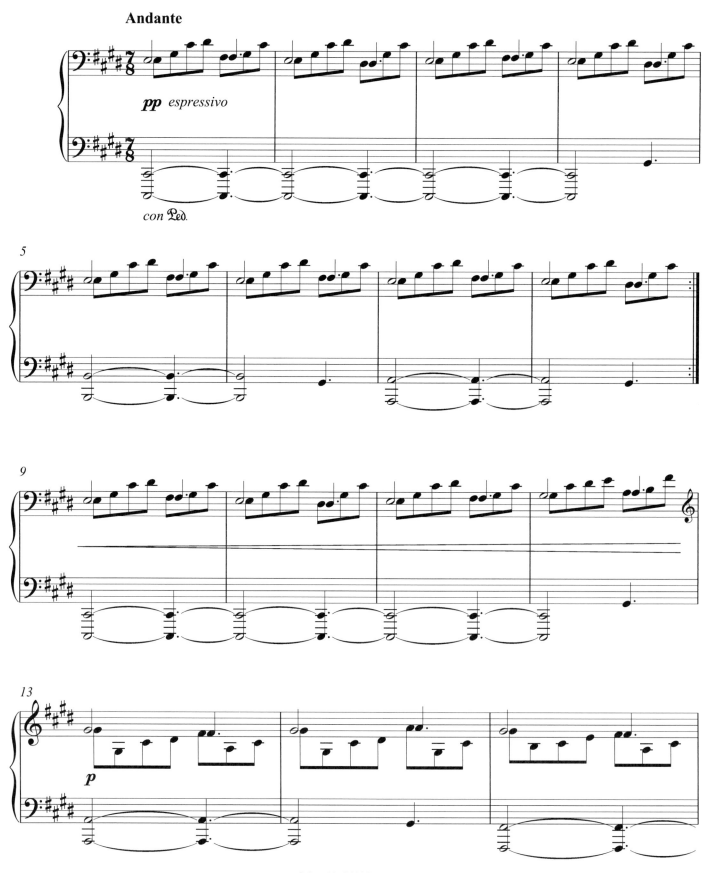

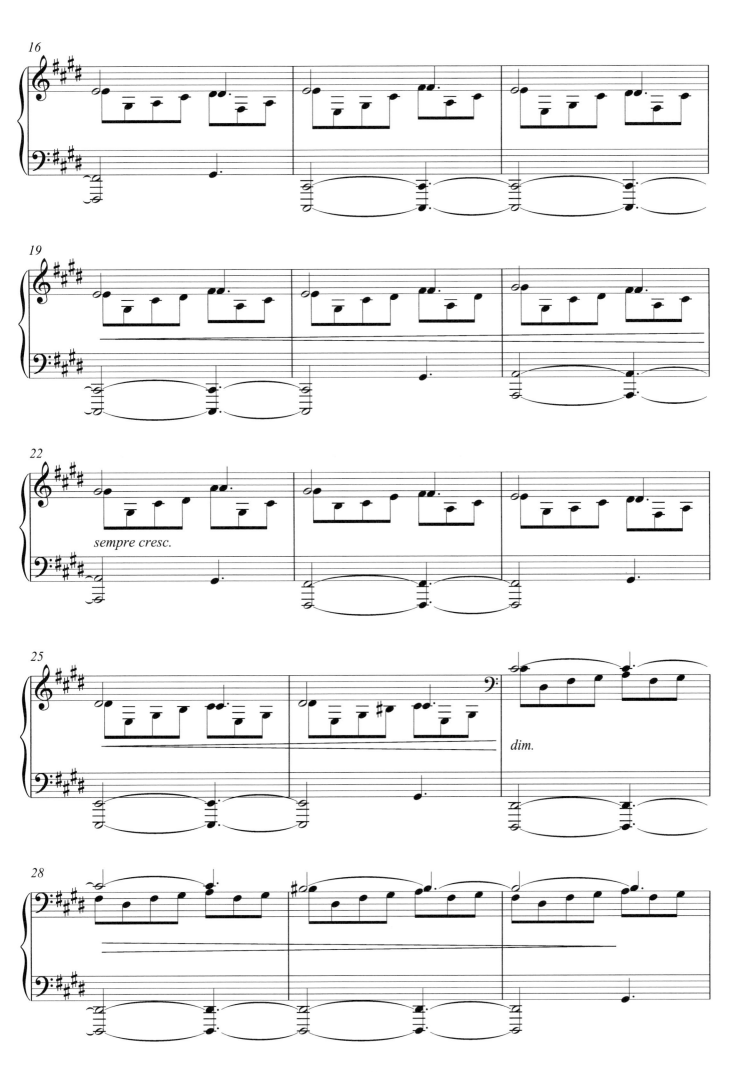

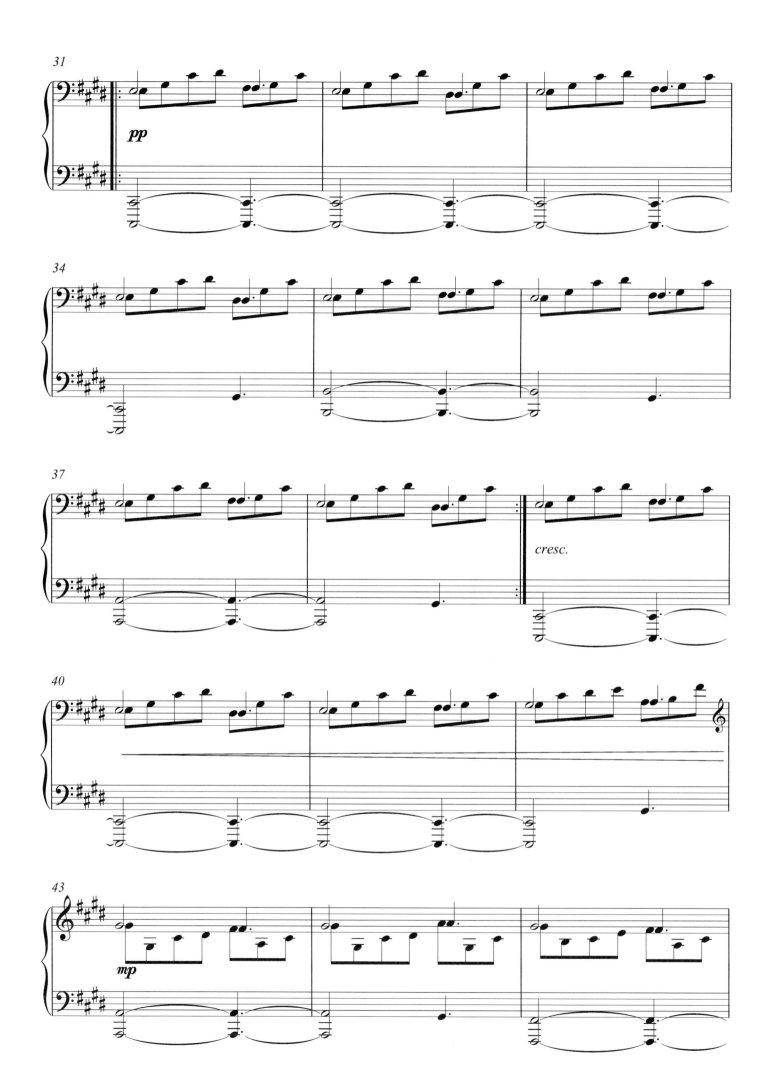

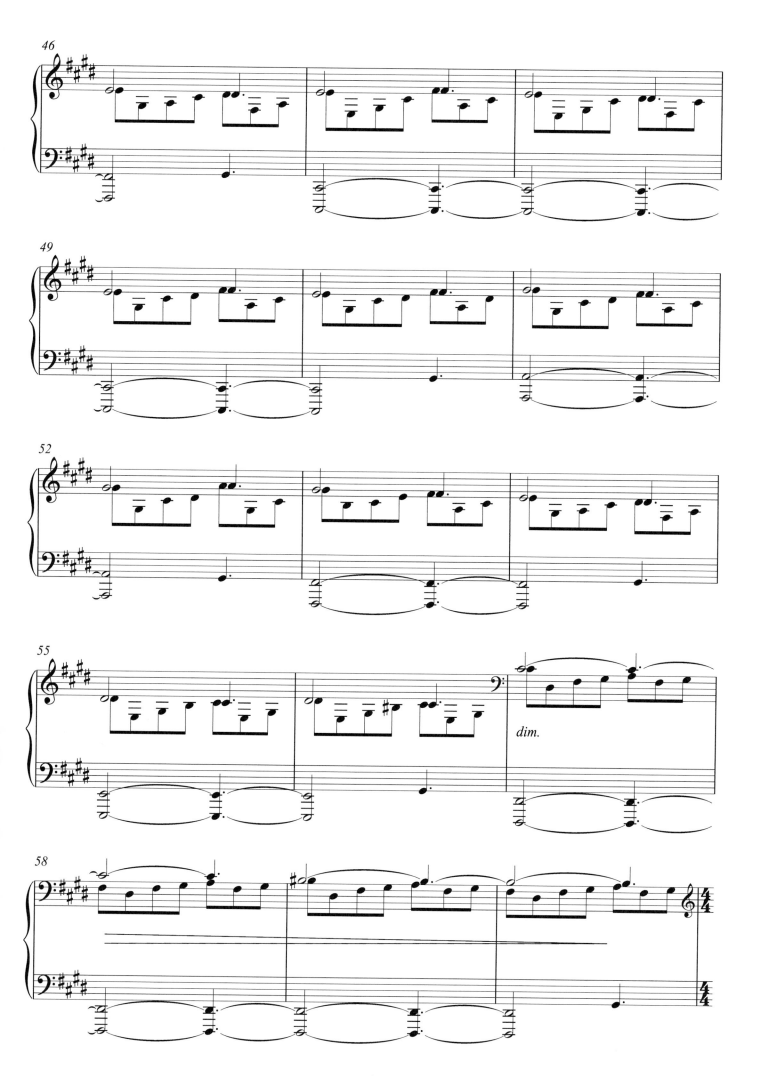

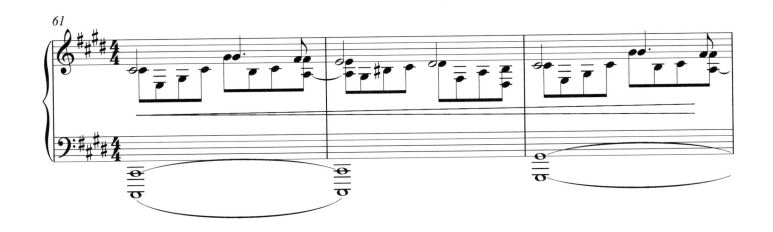

THE BLUE NOTEBOOKS

MUSIC BY MAX RICHTER

CIRCLES FROM THE RUE SIMON-CRUBELLIER

MUSIC BY MAX RICHTER

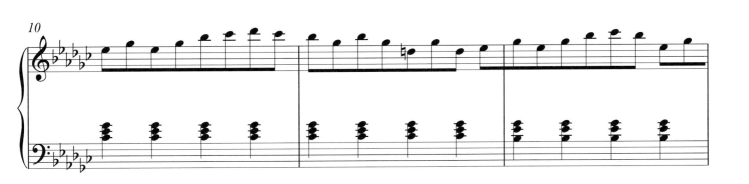

DEPARTURE

MUSIC BY MAX RICHTER

THE FAMILY

MUSIC BY MAX RICHTER

cresc. poco a poco

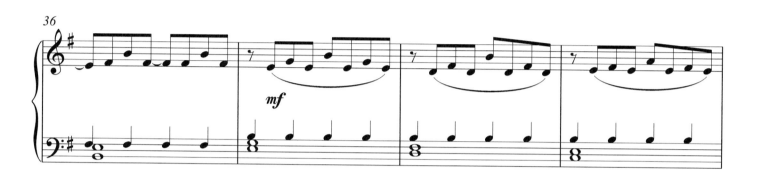

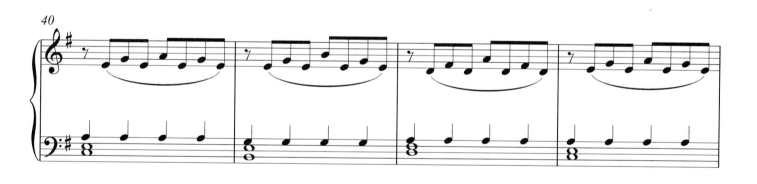

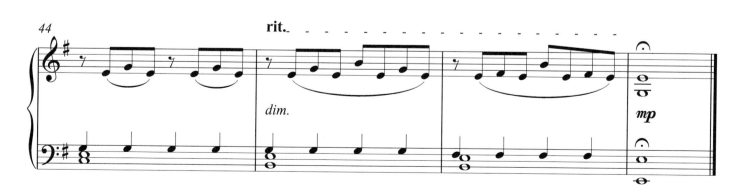

FRAGMENT

MUSIC BY MAX RICHTER

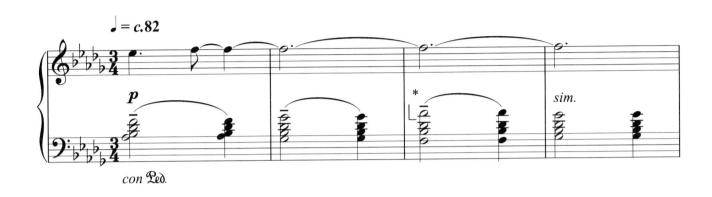

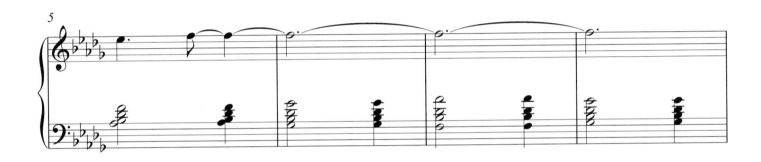

* RH play top note if necessary.

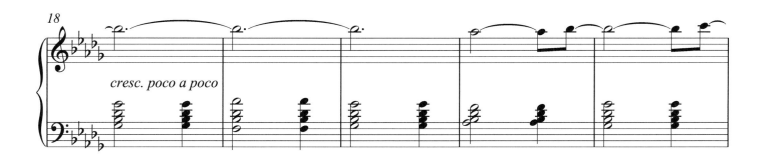

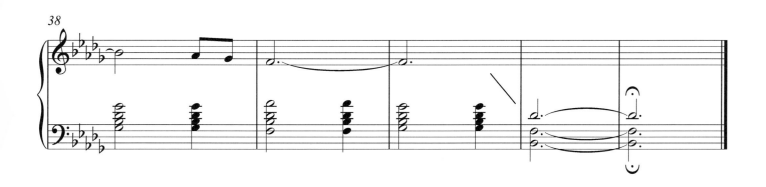

FROM THE RUE VILLIN

MUSIC BY MAX RICHTER

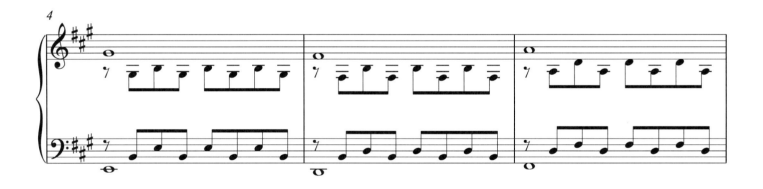

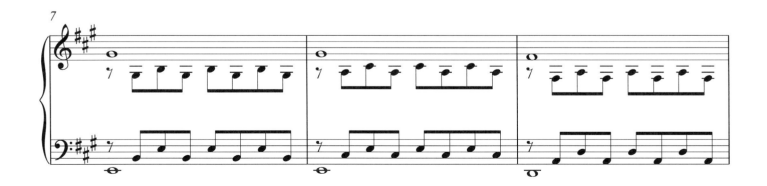

H IN NEW ENGLAND

MUSIC BY MAX RICHTER

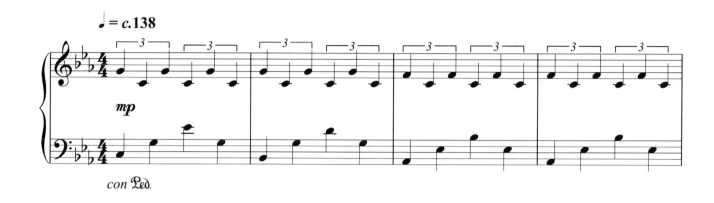

HORIZON VARIATIONS

MUSIC BY MAX RICHTER

poco rit.

INFRA 3

MUSIC BY MAX RICHTER

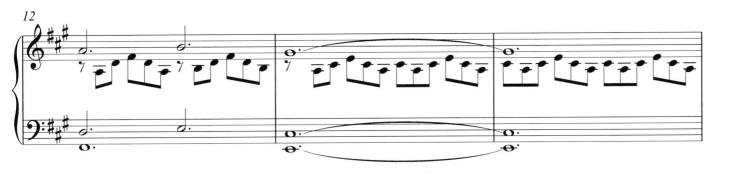

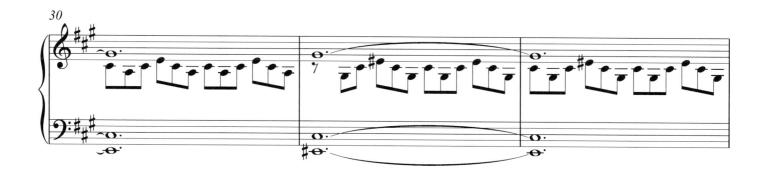

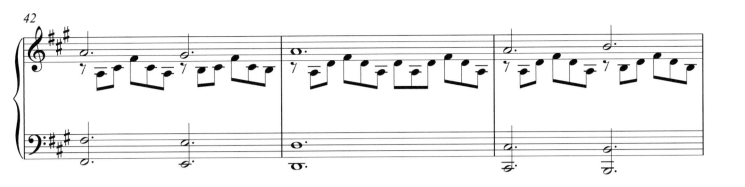

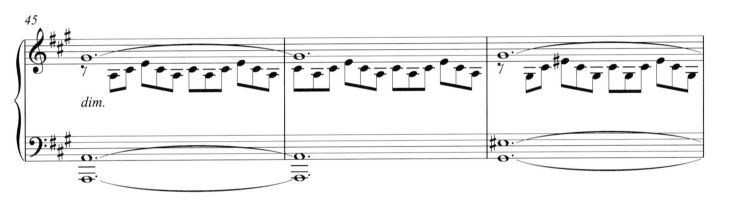

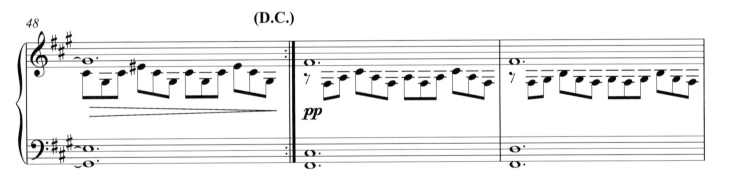

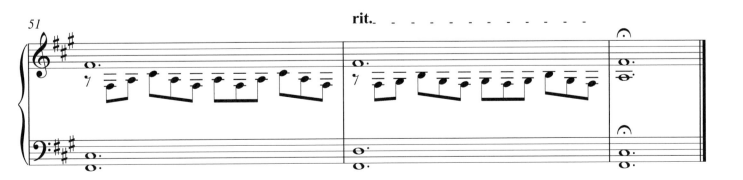

LEO'S JOURNAL

MUSIC BY MAX RICHTER

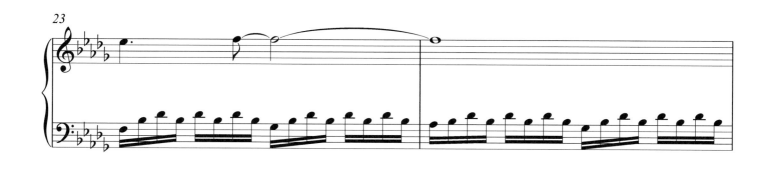

(sempre cresc.)

mp

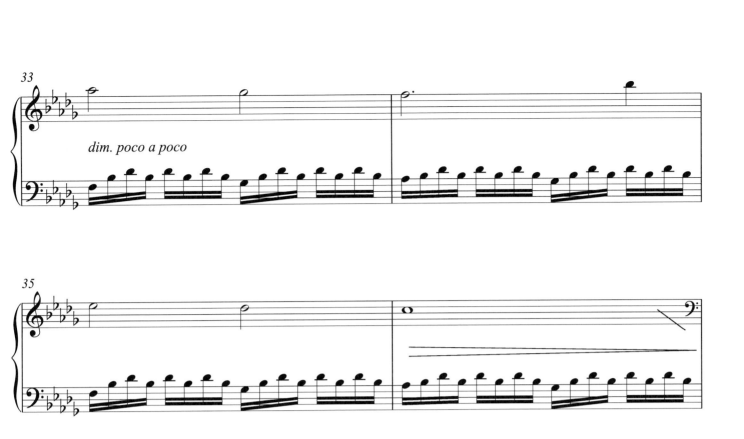

THE TARTU PIANO

MUSIC BY MAX RICHTER

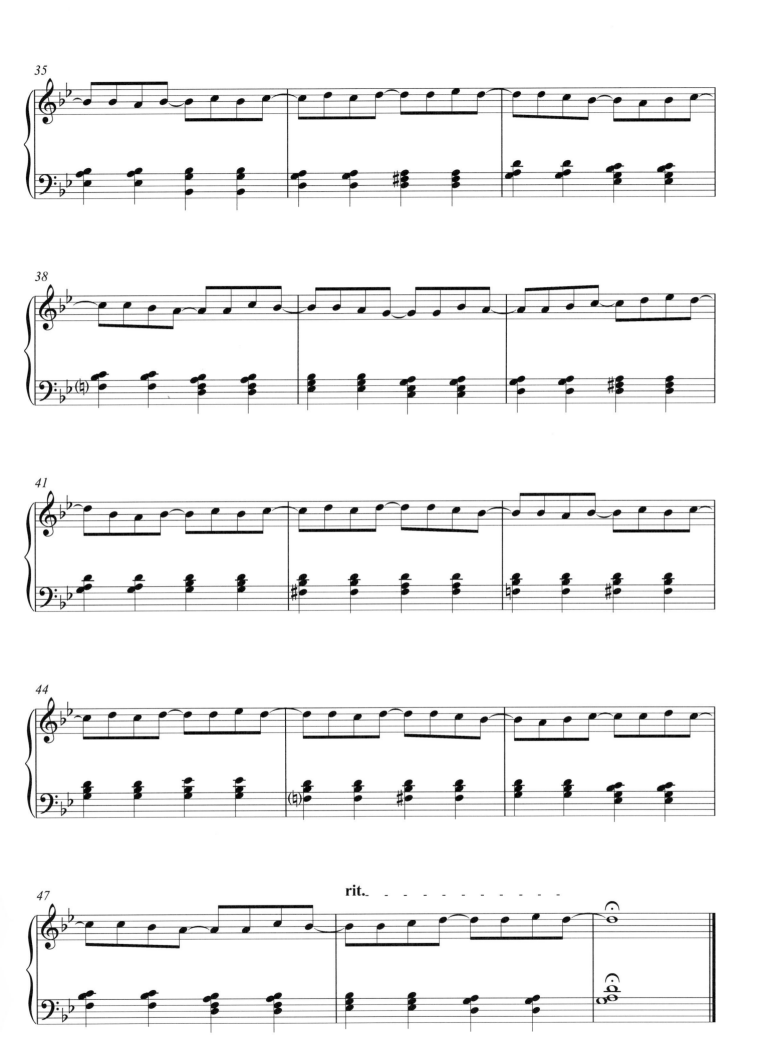

43

THE TWINS (PRAGUE)

MUSIC BY MAX RICHTER

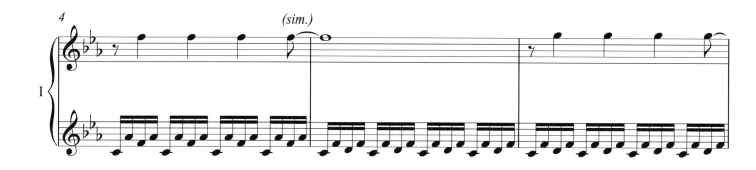

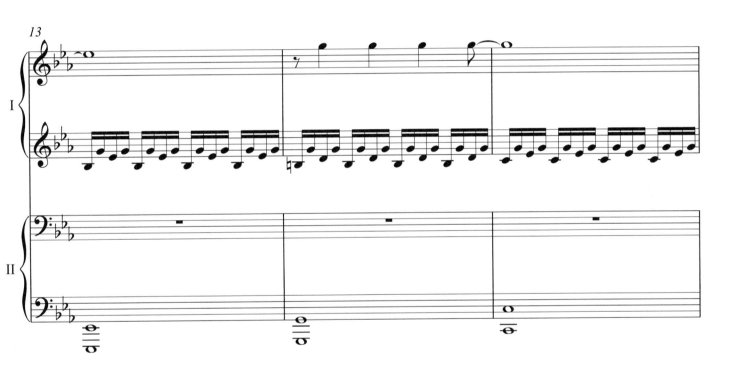

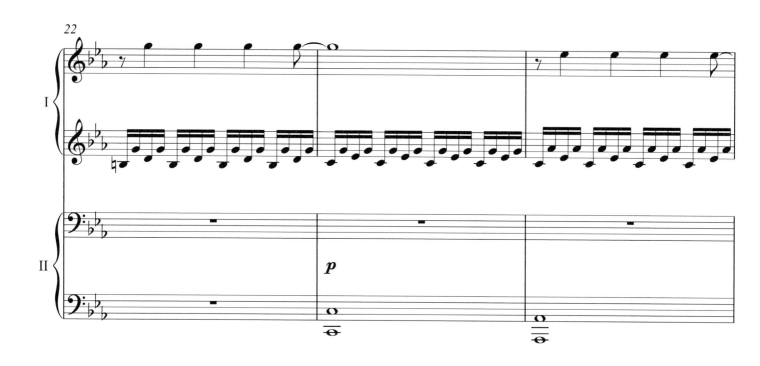

VLADIMIR'S BLUES

MUSIC BY MAX RICHTER

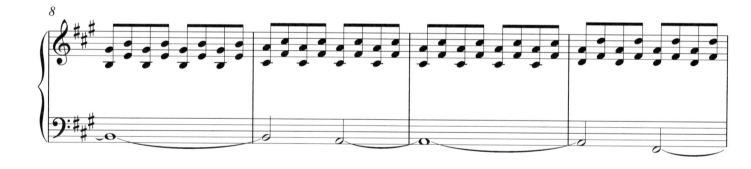

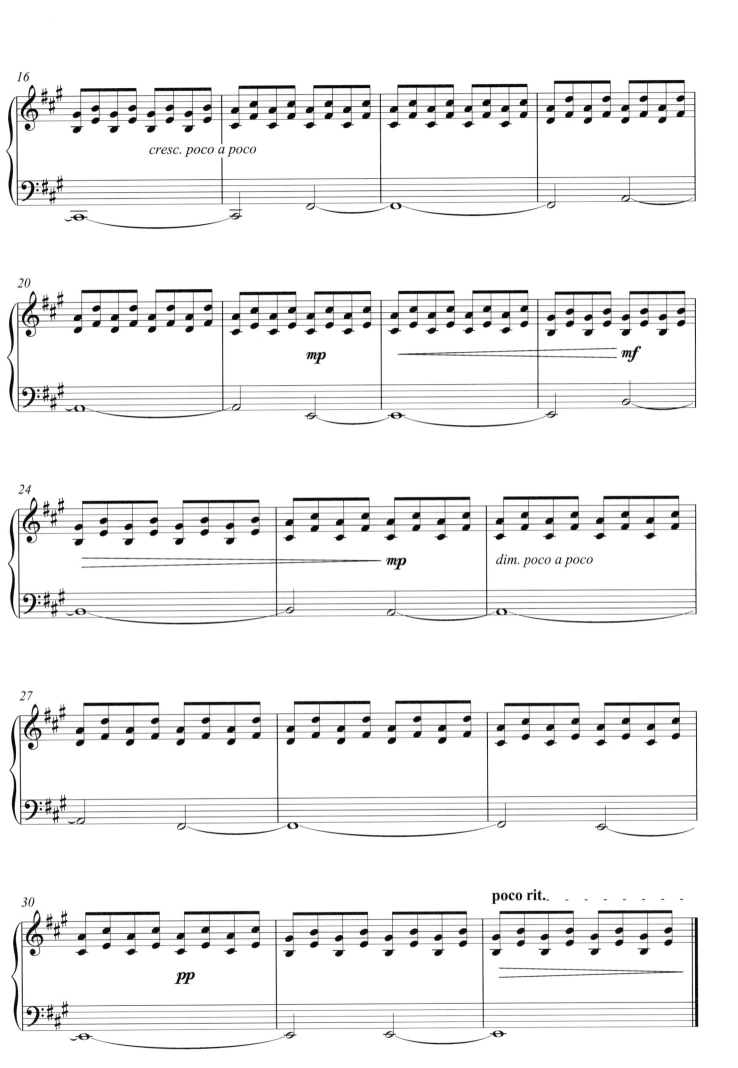

WRITTEN ON THE SKY

MUSIC BY MAX RICHTER

più cresc.

mf *mp*

dim. poco a poco

p *(sempre dim.)*

pp